D1082638

indigo

F. D. SOUL

Indigo

by

f.d.soul

Copyright © 2016 F. D. Soul

All rights reserved.

ISBN: 0473-41140-7

ISBN-13: 978-047341140-4

IN
DI
GO

A POETRY SERIES

by F. D. SOUL

For my mother,
who feels invariably like home

for my father,
who bears the same marrow as I do

and for Chloë

(never stop giving out
oceans)

A poet's guide to healing:

write the things that hurt.

CONTENTS

Part 1:

Skin of Brick & a Breaking Heart

f.d.soul

indigo

There will come a
time when you will
live

- beautifully,
ecstatically live –

rather than
simply
survive.

f.d.soul

The forest fires of today

Inhale my ashes
and make as if
you do not see
the rubble

cannot feel
the wreckage of me

someone once told me
that
"the forest fires of today
lead to the forests
of tomorrow"

please, my love
tell me
you have patience

indigo

let's take these
third-degree burns
and pretend I am a redwood.

f.d.soul

I write because it hurts.
because I need it to hurt.
because it hurts in the
most beautiful way possible.

(because it hurts like you)

indigo

In the attic of me

Perhaps he will never love me
as you could
but he will also
not have the capacity
to feel pain
quite so very deeply

my children
will not be born into
feeling every damn thing
so very tenderly

and perhaps I will never
be able to
not love you

you will always be
there
broken into small pieces
tucked away
in a forgotten draw

f. d. soul

in the attic of me

but perhaps
one day
the leaving of you
will not
hurt
quite this very badly.

indigo

Magnetism

Do you realise
that the marrow of me
is iron oxide
and stepped-on shells

a black beach?

and you;
you and that
ferrous smile

that breaks my very bones.

f. d. soul

The thing about silence
is that it has a heartbeat

has lungs

and all those other
violent, in-between
things.

indigo

As if it were about the words

The people that say
you write well
well
as if
it were about the words
and how
pretty
they look strung together
neatly
against the skin
at your throat
as if
you weren't
standing in front of them
naked

these are the ones that will
suddenly
make you feel
frightfully inadequate
clothed.

f.d.soul

The art of inhaling

The art
of inhaling

as if it were on purpose;

the way that
sometimes
you must be halfway
drowned

before you remember
how to breathe.

indigo

There's a certain pain
behind the eyes.
a stabbing below the ribs.
reserved
for those people
that do not want you
back.

Kindness and its shades

And what would you have
had me do?

put on
an endless blue-sky smile
pat your hand
whisper "it's okay

even though it hurts
to my bones
it's okay"

because in my eyes
I did the kindest thing

we were
breaking each other
and the cracks were forming
faster than we could heal them

indigo

and it was beautiful
and vulnerable
but

eventually one of us would
end up in ruins
and I think that you thought
I left you
so that it would be you.

(I left you
so that it would be me)

f.d.soul

Dead Lights

We watched all those little
dead lights
burning up the sky

(memories
like ours on the grass
between us;
an ashtray)

and we pressed the cold
between our palms
and your skin had never felt
so far away

(I wanted to count
the atoms)

and I wondered how many
of those dying planets
had burnt out long ago

indigo

how it would be months
before either of us noticed

how really, we were just
sitting on the cold ground,
smiling up at ash.

f.d.soul

I had no idea
that smile of yours
would become
my noose.

indigo

Something Else

I would have been
a writer.
a feeler.
a true suede-and-leather
lost soul. a girl
who
breathed music and cigarettes
and indigo
up against the glass at 2am.

maybe I would bite my nails and
claim to have no home
(but for in your arms).
run from the
loneliness in my bed.
see if
I could find it in someone else's.

hold hands more often.
kiss strangers.

f.d.soul

carry that wildness in my eyes
that says
ARTIST.

rust away in the corner with my
typewriter.

frown and drink vodka and
tell the soft wood of the bar stool
about how
I hate my day job.

how I should have chosen
Something Else.

been someone else.

(I would have been a writer)

indigo

f.d.soul

A confession:
it doesn't always melt
off the bones like it should.

indigo

"All you are to me now
is poetry."

(how to tell
exactly when it is
that you've lost the love
of a writer)

As if sorrow were a cold

I lay there with the grass
and the darkness
and you;
you told me
about the stars and about how

sometimes everything hurt
and your breath felt close
enough to catch
(as if sorrow were a cold)

and maybe I should have
shared my lips with yours
but

I was being selfish
that night
and the dirt was digging
into my ribs

indigo

"I'm sorry"
has a habit
of never sounding loud enough

but,
all the same.

f.d.soul

indigo

From across the silence

All those words
welling up in your eyes
and
all I could look at
was the damn water
curling around the stones
like smoke
like raised voices

all that *I'm sorry*
screaming at me from
across the silence

and I was angry
because I couldn't stop it all
blurring
leaking down my chin
bruising the seatbelt

I remember thinking
that autumn is

f.d.soul

my favourite season

so then why are these leaves
all so
damn green

and they just kept falling down
down
down
in that way that leaves do

you reached over then
touched my hand as if
you hardly remembered
my skin
as if
testing my proximity
checking the front door
for my shoes

we kept driving after that

of course we kept driving

indigo

what else can you do

when you love someone
terribly guilty
of being only human.

f.d.soul

The cavity in my chest

How is it that we love
so very much harder
when there is nothing left?

just empty hands
like shells,
and cracked-open hearts

and that deep shade of bruise;
blood on asphalt

(the cavity in my chest)

indigo

Irreversibly so

And
as it turns out

while my tongue
lay dormant and
unable to utter
those feeble words
that you ached for

you were breaking
at the hand of my silence.

irreversibly so.

f.d.soul

A sad reality:

often to cease being lovers
is to become strangers.

indigo

Tell me

I

Tell me about how
he kissed you

the one with the hard hands

how he tasted
like anger
like a clenched jaw

how you had wanted it
(your eyes
had said so!)

how you pushed him away
but you had wanted it

II

Tell me about the boy

who sat on the steps with you

who ran his hand up
up
under your skirt

who felt like ice

about how you'd never before
realised how very shy
your skin was

and how very much
it belonged to you

III

Tell me about the boy
who held you
hands and waist

and neck

indigo

how it wasn't natural
to be so timid

impolite, actually

how he seemed the type
to be aroused by fear

inhaled it in gasps

and so you said
(gently, of course)

"I'm tired, can I go home now?"

instead of

"get the fuck off me."

f.d.soul

For Aleppo

Tell me;
did they fall
like rubble

like rose petals

naked
and grieving
and alone?

indigo

It is then

When you can see her
with your eyes
closed
catch her up
in your empty hands
find her silence
at the back of your throat
when
every Sunday
smells like her hair
and
the grass and the ocean
and the rain
make you miss her
it is then that
you have
known her.

(it is then that
you have
loved her).

f.d.soul

indigo

Chloë

Rest your forehead
against the pen
spill out
the words then
blot yourself dry

always
keep them close
let them ring in your ears
a while
hate them every time
you remember

swear on your life
that you'll forget

but

don't you dare
ever
unlearn

39

f.d.soul

how to love
in that ferocious way
that you do.

indigo

Funny how easily
his eyes
make wounds
out of scars

(funny how readily
his mouth
makes it feel
like healing)

f.d.soul

Fault lines

She traced his veins;
fault lines
across his pale skin
and she wondered
how he could be
so dead
in the eyes
how holding him
felt like
holding broken bones

when life pumped
so vividly
through him.

indigo

f.d.soul

Growing daisies

Perhaps the worst part
was losing the smile
of a happy little girl
who didn't know any better

and wanting ever so much
to go back to where it
had dropped out of her
pocket and find it again

probably trapped in one
of those cracks in the
pavement growing daisies.

indigo

The skin of you

If I trace these words
run my eyes over them
like hands
right across the skin of you
often enough
then perhaps I will learn
you
like braille
like there isn't an ocean
between us
and then when I tell you
my heart is too full
of you
to fit anyone else in
you will wrap your fingers
around this gift
curl the fear up into your palm
and tell me
that you trust me.

f.d.soul

The aerodynamics of flying

I always wondered the
difference between
the aerodynamics of
flying
and me; always
falling
always
irresistibly falling.

indigo

Thank God for
the stubbornness
of organs.

f.d.soul

Part 2:

The Mending of Veins

f.d.soul

indigo

Like home again

It held me
the way that water curls
around your toes and buries
your feet slowly
(unnoticeably slowly)

the way that his arms
curled
around my width

the way his hands dissolved
the fear that held tight
to my hips

and slowly
(immeasurably slowly)

I began to feel
like home again.

f.d.soul

Tipuna:
Te Koeti Turanga

Tūrangawaewae:
my mother

(despite what you think
of my skin.)

indigo

Surely, never alone

I don't think you knew,
even then.
you weren't used to yourself yet.
not alone

surely,
never alone

and I think he told you
it was love

but

he had a way of making
the inside air
too tight

a sharpness
in the back of the eyes

f.d.soul

I remember asking if
you were afraid

and you told me how you wanted
to move to New York
take up painting

have money
and a man that didn't
spend it all

a love that didn't pinch
quite so hard
under the arms.

he left on a Monday.

so it goes.

he left on a November Monday
and I'd like to say that I
was sorry

but I held your hands

indigo

pressed our bones together
so tight
that your hair tickled my mouth

and I noticed
how little you felt like afraid

and I'm sorry for smiling,
but God
your bones felt so free.

f.d.soul

indigo

The most heartbreaking
of truths:

you were loved
long
before you learnt
that there was
an alternative.

Like a white flag

I knew him
for the way he stretched out
his fingers
as we walked
as if he would hold the air
between us

as if he could feel the
pulse
of the dirt
beneath our trainers

he weighed up his words
in his hands
testing their cadence
against his palms

offered them out to me

like a question

indigo

like a white flag

and his eyes,
which were something like
fear,
were also a lot like love

and so,
(of course)

I jumped.

I have a talent for
twisting my tongue
into silence
as tight as a fist
(like a cherry stem)

like fear.

indigo

You were the one that
irresistibly fractured
my soul

(and maybe that's
why I savour
my brokenness)

Heavier than my whole

I think if you broke me up
my pieces would be
heavier
than my whole.
when it came down to it
when you held
fragments of me
in the softness of your hands
and tilted your head to the side
in that way that you do.
taking my measure.
I think that perhaps you would
find me to be
assembled
by arms much stronger
than my own.

indigo

Some days you
must let the words
be water.

f.d.soul

Every ounce

I don't know which
words will tell you
that your smile
is infinitely more beautiful
than your bones, love.
but it is.
with every ounce of honesty
in this body,
it is.

indigo

Of course
it had to hurt –

how else would we
have realised how
beautiful it was?

This land is my church

See over there
between the trees
where the light blinks
stained glass windows
and

the sun
waves good morning,
how are you this fine Sunday
would you like a newsletter
and

the grass bows
into that soft carpet
the type that's
hard to move chairs on
and

the soft white of
the clouds will tumble
over you

indigo

the pastor's words
the smile of his wife
and

you will inhale the air
and close your eyes
feel the stillness
against your palms
and

of course,
then there is always
the food
the tea
the breaking of bread

you can be sad
lonely
as defeated as you like
but there will always be
the bread.

f.d.soul

indigo

But see; how
moved
are the trees
by the wind.

f. d. soul

The call of the tawny owl

I'd like to think
that it is
the voice of his mother

that
when he was born inside
a dead tree
broke his way out
she whispered to him

that she handed him
vernacular
like a gift

like an apology.

indigo

I want your breath
tattooed in my lungs.

f.d.soul

Pieces

I'm sorry if you find
pieces of me in your bed
and in your shirts
and in your hair

in that light that flickers
gently by your front door

and the smell of coffee and toast
and warm mornings

because the truth is
I lost myself with you
and you'll probably find
my left-behind pieces
scattered like bobby pins

and I can't even say that
I'm sorry for that

indigo

for here;
I have your pieces too.

f.d.soul

I just want you
to know
that I wouldn't
for a second
take any of it back.

How to read poetry

Think of
how your lungs feel
after that first jump
into the sea
when everything
pulls you tightly
inwards

how
inhaling smoke
reminds you of
the forest that was
but also
how good
a fire feels at the back
of your throat

and know
that these are her bones
her bare feet

f.d.soul

the dust that stuck to
the sweat of her forehead
last July

(who gives a damn
about the words?)

indigo

Find yourself. In the stillness between your
breaths. In the softness of your hands. Find
yourself and don't you dare ever let go.

f.d.soul

What it was to live

He had beautifully frightening ideas
about what it was to live

and he was terrifying
delightfully terrifying
in the way he danced through it all

caught it
on his tongue

laughed into
the wind

turned your face upwards
with his hands
as if to catch the rain

as if to say

"look, here.
just look at the loveliness of it all."

78

indigo

The way my skin
leans towards him

like an inhale;

he holds gravity in
those eyes
I swear.

f.d.soul

As if

There was something in
those eyes of hers.

a burning,
terrified sort of laughter.

as if she feared that
she wouldn't be able
to hold back her smile.

as if she feared that
she would.

indigo

Do not ever let agony
get comfortable beneath your skin

- you are not a home for heartbreak

Why you are afraid

Show them your scars
when they ask why you are afraid

when you tell them that
perhaps
they will fall hopelessly
out of love with you

and they laugh
"baby, please"
and kiss you on your forehead

the same spot
they use to say
goodbye

show them that
you wear the soft handprints
of a single mother

like the loveliest of scars

indigo

tell them that
they are a bull in a china shop

that you fear
marrying into infidelity
could be genetic

and,
dear one,

here's the worst
most beautiful part of it all:
they will tell you that they love you

and all you can do
is hope to God that they mean it.

f.d.soul

indigo

How exhilarating;
to discover the strength
in one's softness.

f.d.soul

Be gentle
on your
lungs.
forgive them
in great sobs
when you must.

indigo

On breaking and entering

Claim me in the way
that the ocean softly
breaks back
the umber cliffs
by my home

in the way that the sky
folds up its corners
traces out the curves
of the northern lights

claim me with
a question mark

with a blank page
that smells like the spine
of an old book
like pine needles
and safety

f.d.soul

claim me
with a hand offered.

indigo

How beautiful it is
to be fragile and
broken and
loved all at once.

f.d.soul

Into the folds of you

Tell me where your skin
has been. who
it holds and held and will.
press it to mine.
tuck my breath into
the folds of you.
catch me up against the length of you.
let me trace the earth
of your home.

indigo

I can't tell you how much
I need you to see me.

f.d.soul

Everything that was us

I will fill my hands with
these moments. white knuckled
I will hold them. push them
into my pockets.
press them
between book pages.
tuck them under my mattress.
hang them
upside-down in the hot water
cupboard until they crinkle at the
touch
of my fingers. until
they turn pastel and sepia and
faded at
all of their edges
and then
everything that was
(everything that was us)
will stay.

indigo

You are
the most beautiful
stranger
I have ever had
the pleasure of
knowing.

The art of floor staring

I

Break softly but
pull the band-aid off
all at once
soak before scrubbing
notice the redness
rub your eyes
some more
but always take
someone with you

II

Tuck your hair back
behind your ears
before your mother
does it for you
before you have a chance
to relearn the art
of hiding
of floor staring

indigo

III

Apathy is
yesterday's gum
spit out
the taste of indifference
rub your shoes on
the gravel
put your head
out the window
test the wind with your hair

remember
how wildly in love you are
with all of this.

f.d.soul

Close your eyes, darling;
your heart is showing

indigo

f.d.soul

My love, you
have no idea of the
power you hold
in those soft little hands
of yours.

Guitar strings and faded pages

There is a lot to be said
for guitar strings
and faded pages

my cousin used to get nosebleeds
and now every novel
she owns
every well-thumbed
chapter holds a few
blood cells
an exasperated sigh
and a quickly pressed
handkerchief

it is weight
and warmth on fingers
that feels like a smile
like cold nights
in jackets and arms

f.d.soul

like sand and burning driftwood
and singing with the sigh
of the waves.

indigo

Fall.
as many times
as it takes,
fall.

f.d.soul

102

indigo

The hard part wasn't letting
go; the hard part was knowing
you would never again be able
to hold on without fear.

f.d.soul

In the wet of the ashes

It's a bushfire to think it was
your fault,
I'll tell you that now.

and it won't be
until you're lying in the underbrush
grieving
in the wet of the ashes
at the foot
of a skeleton forest

that you'll realise.

indigo

We are thieves,
all of us,
in this rebellion
we call 'art'

f.d.soul

Eyes of his

It was because
I saw myself,

reflected in those
midnight eyes
of his,

that I tried
so very hard
to love him.

indigo

I will tell you this
again and again
and again;
you are enough.

you are so incredibly
enough.

f.d.soul

The bravest thing

The bravest thing
she ever did
was to live

and perhaps
the most dangerous thing

(the most beautiful)

was to hope.

indigo

Think of all the weather
worn
by you
by your skin
now
look at the softness
and how it stays.

f.d.soul

Torrential salt

She tasted of the sea,
and when he sat close enough
he could watch the gulls
circling in her eyes;
see the ocean
leaking down her
canyon-carved cheeks.

and he learnt the spot
on her neck
where it would collect
like lost shells

where he could press
his mouth
to save her from
drowning in
all that
torrential salt.

indigo

Tell me
how do you give yourself
back to someone

and

what if
(especially if)
that someone is you?

f.d.soul

Pin down your heavy eyelids child;
catch the stars
in your lashes
and the night
in your lungs,
and don't you ever let yourself
grow too old for dreaming.

To hell with what they think.
smile your beautiful smile,
and speak your beautiful truth.

be undeniably you.

f.d.soul

Part 3:

Bare Feet & Universe Breathing

f.d.soul

indigo

Life

It's really just a lot
of losing
and finding
and loving
and hurting

an endless process of
breaking and unbreaking
ourselves

but God, it's so beautiful.

f.d.soul

Small talk

She was never very good at
small talk

her heart was much too big
her eyes too wide

she could pour her soul
into the palm of your hand
and teach you how to feel

but for the life of her
she could not ask
and truly care
what the weather chose to do.

indigo

Always inwards

There is bravery
in the way you sip your tea
sweet
in the way you fold
yourself
inwards
always inwards
like Japanese paper art
in the way
you tie your shoes
and take that first inhale
of outside air

in the way you love

in the way you faultlessly
love.

f.d.soul

So long as they
never take
my
peace.

Kaleidoscope

Of course you feel at home
in the grass beneath
those stars

this world is noise
and
colour
and
universe

just like you.

f.d.soul

She healed in such a way
that she fell in love with
herself all over again.

indigo

Call it a scar

It seems that these cells
this carpet over my bones
that once creaked
under the weight of you
will last only weeks

and I cannot decide
if it is a blessing or curse
(perhaps it is enough
to simply call it
a scar)
that these neurons
that once smiled against
your mouth

remain.

f.d.soul

Meanderer

There is nothing wrong
with being a meanderer
so long as you make
certain that your shoes
are getting dirty
and your face freckled.

indigo

Deeply,
inexplicably,
irrevocably –

that is how you deserve to be loved.

f.d.soul

indigo

2am and then some

She remembered it because of the floor-length
dress. because of the way it whispered around
her thighs and played gently with the gravel by
her feet.

because she wasn't used to having her hand feel
safe in someone else's.

but it did.

she would watch him when he wasn't looking.
when he was concentrating on taking tipsy steps
forward.

his thumb brushing absently against her skin

she remembered because the night sky sat in the
harbour, getting drunk with the sleepy boats. on
fermented salt and audacity.

and he dared her to jump in with them.

she nearly did – heels and all. she wasn't used
to vodka, or to having breath so close to her
ear. hands so tight at her waist.

she nearly did.

she only later remembered that she should
have been cautious. afraid, even. to give away
so much of herself.

to press her soul into places where he felt only
skin.

but he had the loveliest of eyes, and too much
confidence for it to be real.

so she stayed.

2am and then some. nothing so inane as
crumpled sheets and avid mouths.

indigo

they sat on a park bench and tossed stories like
stones out into the water. listening with
nervous eyes as they landed. bare feet curled
up against the cold.

ear pressed tight against his chest as if asking
for a second opinion.

he held the door of the taxi when she left.
waited before ordering his. each inhaling the
stillness between them, warmed from the
asphalt.

and perhaps if she hadn't remembered in that
very moment to be afraid,

she might have pressed her lips against his.

she nearly did.

f.d.soul

indigo

There's something about
brokenness
that isn't as bad
as they make it out to be.

f.d.soul

A note for Steve

Have you ever thought
that perhaps
you fill your world
with art
because to you
that is what
home feels like

because anything worth
feeling
should be felt in
exquisite colour and
feverish detail

because life
is all the more captivating
filled with beautiful,
painful things

(because me too)

indigo

But where would
courage be,
without fear?

f.d.soul

You can say a lot with silence
like
I think that maybe
I loved you
and I'm sorry it came out
as goodbye
and what I wouldn't give
to tell you
how beautiful you were
and are
and will be.

indigo

How to stand without swaying

He was the shore,
goodness knows he was the shore
after a life spent out at sea
when you have long
forgotten
the smell of grass and how
to stand without swaying
and then
suddenly your lips are
pressed
up against that cool dry earth
and you don't know
why you're crying
but every sailor's song
makes sense now
and God,
the ground never tasted
so good.

f.d.soul

indigo

Be that wind that
carries
with it the
rain;
bearing
forever bearing.

f.d.soul

You make damn sure

Sometimes your breath will catch
and you'll feel it all pour back
(all those things
you worked so hard to grow out of)
and that's okay.

blow it back out
before it sticks to the inside
of your lungs.

curse at it, if that helps.

cry a little.

but you make damn sure it knows
how unwelcome it is.

indigo

The beautiful,
wretched truth
is that we're all
still hurting.

There was something
in her fingertips that
they didn't understand

a yearning
like an itch

to feel
and be felt;

pain or otherwise

indigo

f.d.soul

It is not
the way they look
but the way
they *see*
that you will
fall in love with.

indigo

When you must listen

When the sky is sleepy grey
and blinking
and the 6am grass crunches
still
that is when
you must listen
for there will be such
a quietness
while they all sleep
'cept for the birds
'cept for you
and you will hear your heart
murmur
good morning
and oh,
it will be.

f.d.soul

I've always found that *home* is simply
a matter of carrying it with you.

indigo

Anything other

It was like
breathing sunlight
to kiss her

(the way she poured
herself into you)

and nothing that
vulnerable
could be made

for anything other
than love.

f.d.soul

Swallow me up
into your laughing eyes
and I will
relinquish all rights
to this heart.

indigo

How very human

Burn bright with all
that you know, little heart.

burn bright with all
that you love

all that you fear

keep these warm
in your hot little hands

because one day
you will need to be reminded
of just
how very human
you are.

f.d.soul

You will break
more times than you
can count,
but you will heal

beautifully
beautifully
beautifully.

indigo

Indigo

I

(photoperiodic induction)

chrysanthemums
and strawberries
will only ever
bloom
when the nights
grow long enough
cold enough
and rugged
so stare at
the inside of your eyelids
a while
take a fistful of
everything you squint against
and find
your flowers

indigo

II

(on why it's never dark in Alaska)

sixty-seven days of
dusk
and yet
you can still stoke
the fire
rub the chill from
your bones
write poetry
wait
for the sunlight months
(which will always
last longer)
taste the smoke but
still
breathe

III

(because darkness is broken)

151

f.d.soul

they will tell you
that darkness is
absence
darkness is broken
and you
you will turn your face
up
to the stars
up against the wind
and notice
however gently that you must
that the night
was only ever pitch
when it was stretched out
leading
and how lovely were
the stars
how kind
that the night sky
(at worst)
was really only ever
indigo.

ABOUT THE AUTHOR

Jamie Louise (pen name F. D. Soul) is a New Zealand author and poet.

Really, she's just another stray human searching for the words to describe the 'ugh' she feels between her ribs.

You can find her on Instagram (@featherdownsoul), or in the garden picking things with her toes and feeding pumpkin to the caterpillars.

A note from her:
thank you to infinity and back

93005381R00105

Made in the USA
San Bernardino, CA
06 November 2018